The Life and Philosophy of
Malcolm
X

The Life and Philosophy of
Malcolm
X

THE **NEW**
HERESA

SANDE SMITH

**CHARTWELL
BOOKS, INC.**

Published by
CHARTWELL BOOKS, INC.
A division of BOOK SALES, INC.
110 Enterprise Avenue
Secaucus, New Jersey 07094

Produced by
Brompton Books Corp.
15 Sherwood Place
Greenwich, CT 06830

ISBN 1-55521-863-6

Printed in Hong Kong

Dedicated to Mildred Smith and
Roosevelt Smith

PAGE 1: Malcolm X at a press
conference held at the Hotel
Theresa in New York City on May
21, 1964. He called for an
alliance of blacks to bring the
plight of African-Americans before
the United Nations.

PREVIOUS PAGES: Whenever he
could, Malcolm exposed police
brutality against black people.
The men in the picture were shot
by police in LA in 1962.

RIGHT: In 1960, Howard University
students marched to the Capitol
demanding passage of the
proposed Civil Rights Bill.

TABLE OF CONTENTS

Introduction

"Once he is motivated, no one can change more completely than the man who has been to the bottom. I call myself the best example of that." From Malcolm Little to Malcolm X to El-Hajj Malik El-Shabazz, from drug addict to champion for black people's rights all over the world, Malcolm X's life demonstrates sweeping spiritual growth.

As Malcolm Little, he was an addict hooked on marijuana and cocaine, making a living by hustling and stealing. He didn't value his life or anyone else's. Arrested and sentenced to ten years in prison, he came face to face with the emptiness of his life. Aided by his family, his eyes and mind opened to the teachings of the Honorable Elijah Muhammad. He later explained his submission to Allah: "When you take one step toward Allah, Allah takes two steps toward you." So began Malcolm's spiritual journey.

While in prison, Malcolm became a voracious reader, studying up to fifteen hours a day. He joined the prison debating team, thrilled by thinking on his feet, publicly overturning his opponent's arguments. During this time, Malcolm began his almost fanatical documentation and exposure of the white man's systematic brutality against black people.

As Malcolm X, he grew strong within the Nation of Islam. After a few years of dedicated service, he became the first man awarded the title National Minister. He expanded the Nation's message to one of black nationalism, that encouraged black people to take their destiny into their own hands and to recognize their link with the fates of black people the world over. Not content to see American blacks fight only for civil rights, he urged that they fight for human rights, and that they take the United States before an international court – the United Nations.

He was not to stay with the Nation of Islam. After his painful break with the Nation in 1964, he set out on his own, travelling to Mecca out of devotion to Allah. He returned as El-Hajj Malik El-Shabazz, an orthodox Sunni Muslim, even more staunchly in favor of black people internationalizing their struggle. He no longer taught that whites were "devils," but his demands that white people take collective responsibility for their role as oppressors of blacks continued stronger than ever. He held that whites must prove their humanity with their deeds. Would they treat black people justly and humanely? If not, then black people had the right to defend themselves – "by any means necessary."

Twenty-eight years have passed since Malcolm was shot dead at Harlem's Audubon Ballroom on February 21, 1965. Yet it's as if he just died. His message is more sought after than ever. His speeches can be purchased recorded

ABOVE: Malcolm, along with the Nation of Islam, stressed that black people must give up poisons, such as drugs and alcohol, in order to live productive lives.

RIGHT: A brilliant speaker, Malcolm was unrelenting in his indictment of white America.

RIGHT: Malcolm grants a press conference at Lewis Michaux's National Memorial African Book Store, a gathering place for black nationalists in Harlem. He urged blacks to learn to use shotguns and rifles in order to defend themselves from racist attacks.

Spike Lee's 1992 film *Malcolm X* popularized Malcolm X's life:

LEFT: Spike Lee as Shorty, and Denzel Washington as Malcolm X, in a scene that takes place at Boston's Roseland Ballroom.

BELOW LEFT: Washington as Malcolm X addresses a crowd in Harlem.

BELOW: Delroy Lindo as West Indian Archie (left), with Denzel Washington.

on audiocassettes, and his image is printed on T-shirts. New books describe, interpret and analyze him. Operas have been composed about him, and off-Broadway plays written about him. And Spike Lee's 1992 film *Malcolm X* dramatizes his life.

Rappers, largely responsible for the renaissance of interest in him, sample his voice, transforming his fiery words into the staccato rhythm of rap. Their lyrics call up his warnings, his fierce caring, his demands for justice for the 22 million black people in America. (Since Malcolm's death, that 22 million has become 30 million.) And while some of the conditions that Malcolm rallied against have changed, many remain the same. Because African-Americans still face racially-induced violence and ignorance, his message resonates just as deeply as it did when he lived.

Malcolm X and Martin Luther King, Jr.: in death as in life, these two men's ideologies are weighed against one another. While the ideology of nonviolence espoused by Martin Luther King has been adopted by the American community as a whole, Malcolm's message of justice "by any means necessary" has been almost exclusively claimed and maintained by the African-American community. With the renaissance of interest in his life, however, white people are once again faced with the power of his words. And not just whites, but young blacks, too young to have seen and heard him speak, must figure out the meaning of this man's life and philosophy.

Before Malcolm many blacks did not consider themselves beautiful, or special, or heaven forbid, better than white people. Malcolm rubbed a healing balm on the tattered psyches of black people. His message preceded that of Black power. Hating the term Negro in common usage at the time – he preferred to say black, or Afro-American – he encouraged black people to know their history, and to love themselves as black, as African people.

Malcolm spread the Nation of Islam's command that blacks not integrate with whites. "Let that ugly thing suffer, in his sin and immorality." He scolded black people for their worship of whites. By calling white people "that ugly ole pale thing," he demystified them.

He taught black people to find their own strength in each other, and to turn away from the corruptness and immorality of the United States, which had not only wronged the American black people, but also was poisoning Africa and Asia.

Malcolm despised the turn-the-other-cheek philoso-

LEFT: Dr. Martin Luther King and Malcolm X shake hands during their only meeting, in 1964. They disagreed fervidly on the tactics that blacks should use to gain justice, yet both men admired one another from afar. Years later their daughters, Yolanda King and Attallah Shabazz, would work together in a theater group.

ABOVE: Malcolm signs autographs during a march in Washington, DC in June 1963. Thousands of blacks joined together to demand fair housing and fair employment practices.

LEFT: In Birmingham, Alabama, on May 4, 1963, 3000 people rallied to protest jim crow laws of segregation and discrimination against blacks. These three protesters hold hands against the fierce onslaught of water from riot police.

phy. He preached, do unto others as they have done unto you. An eye for an eye, a tooth for a tooth, a hand for a hand; that was the kind of justice that Malcolm espoused.

He asserted that once white people realized that blacks would no longer stand docilely by while dogs were unleashed on them, their men were burned, their women raped, and their children miseducated, they would be forced to recognize and respect black people's intelligence and power.

Malcolm's sharp wit lanced the festering wound of hypocrisy. He demanded, "How can you make someone a slave and think you're too good to be a slave?" He forced whites to confront their fantasy that blacks adored them and were satisfied to remain in their place, or were at least too scared to tell them different. He was the "crazy nigger" screaming words that whites had lynched black people for whispering.

He confronted white people, holding them accountable for the evil conditions of black people's lives. He pointed out that overpriced housing, poor schooling, easy access to drugs, and corrupt and racist policing all led to overcrowding, social diseases and pathological behavior.

When Malcolm called whites "devils," and compared the "responsible" black civil rights leaders to dogs that guard the master's house, he enraged many. Yet he used his cutting wit to personify the abstract, to make it plain. He knew how to break down the workings of systematic oppression so that the masses of black people could get the message and relate it to their lives.

Reporters called him a hatemonger, yet tantalized by his power and intelligence, they came back for more. Black leaders of the civil rights movement feared he threatened integration and equality among blacks and whites. They tried to ignore him, but his influence spread, even among their followers.

Who was this man, this healer of black people's souls, this relentless seeker of truth willing to pay the ultimate price for justice – death?

Malcolm Little

Malcolm Little was born on May 19, 1925, in Omaha, Nebraska, to Earl and Louise Little. Louise was very light skinned, and could pass for white. Earl was a large, very black man. A Baptist minister, Earl also delivered the message of Marcus Garvey.

Garvey, originally from Jamaica, created the Universal Negro Improvement Association (UNIA), the first extensive black nationalist movement in the United States that appealed to the masses of black people. He envisioned blacks becoming politically, economically, and culturally independent by connecting with one another throughout the world.

Malcolm's parents were driven out of Nebraska by the local equivalent of the Ku Klux Klan. One night Louise heard a knock on the door. Alone with her two children,

and pregnant with Malcolm, she convinced the whites at the door that her husband was away, in order to get them to go away. They left, but not before breaking all the windows in the house.

The family moved to Lansing, Michigan. Soon after they arrived, the house was set afire. Malcolm and his family watched as the house burned to the ground. From there, they moved to East Lansing, Michigan, a small town on the outskirts of Lansing. Despite the clear signs that the local white people did not like "their Negroes" being "riled up," Earl continued to spread the teaching of Marcus Garvey.

In his autobiography, Malcolm said that one of his most vivid childhood memories was of his father taking him to UNIA meetings held in people's homes. Up to 20 people would gather in someone's living room. Because they didn't jump and shout as they did during Earl's Baptist sermons, Malcolm thought they appeared more intelligent and down to earth. At those meetings, his father would promise that it would not be long before Africa would be completely run by black men. People passed around big, shiny photos of Marcus Garvey riding in his fine car, surrounded by throngs of black people. The meetings always closed with Earl saying several times, with the people chanting after him, "Up, you mighty race, you can accomplish what you will!"

All was not peaceful, however, in Malcolm's home.

ABOVE RIGHT: Lansing, Michigan, in 1924.

RIGHT: Night Riders, forerunners of the Black Legion. The Black Legion threatened Earl Little because he preached that black people must stand up for political and economic independence.

LEFT: Marcus Garvey (right), founder and president of the Universal Negro Improvement Association (UNIA) with two UNIA members in 1924.

Earl and Louise fought a lot, and sometimes Earl hit Louise. He also beat the children hard and often – except for Malcolm. Louise usually beat him. In reflecting on this later, Malcolm believed that Earl subconsciously favored him because he was the lightest of Earl's children.

Malcolm recalled the day of his father's death in detail in his autobiography. That afternoon in 1931, Wilfred, Hilda, Philbert and Malcolm came home to find their parents having a fierce argument. Tension had been high in the house, because Earl had received threats from the Black Legion, the local white supremacy group. After killing a rabbit and insisting that Louise cook it for supper even though he knew she hated to eat rabbit, Earl started out of the house. Louise, still crying, had a vision that something was about to happen to Earl. "Early! Early!" she screamed. Earl, already well up the road, turned, waved and continued on his way. Later that night, the children were awakened by Louise's screams. The police

ABOVE: A UNIA parade in Harlem in 1930. UNIA's annual parades and conventions in New York drew thousands. With several hundred chapters around the country, the UNIA was the biggest mass-based nationalist movement among black people to date.

RIGHT: Marcus Garvey raised millions of dollars to carry out his plans for American blacks to establish economic links to Africa and the Caribbean.

had come to tell her that Earl was dead. His beaten body had been found on the trolley car tracks, cut nearly in two. No one was ever indicted for Earl's death.

Louise had eight children to raise, alone and without money. Her husband had been proud that he had bought two insurance policies to provide for his family should anything happen. When Louise tried to collect on the policies, she was only able to collect on the smaller one, for about $1000. Insisting that Earl had committed suicide, the insurance agents would not pay a dime on the larger policy.

This left the family very poor. In his autobiography, Malcolm described day after day of dizzying hunger with only dandelion greens and cornbread to eat. He started arriving at friends' houses at dinner time, gratefully accepting when he was asked to stay.

Eventually Malcolm started to steal because he was so hungry, and also because he wanted a little something for himself. Meanwhile, Louise was forced to apply for welfare. The welfare agents came around regularly, investigating and asking questions. Malcolm remembered them checking up on how Louise was raising her children.

Louise was having a difficult time making ends meet. Every time she found a job, sewing or doing housework in a white household, her employer would discover she was black, or learn that she was the widow of that "crazy" Earl Little, and she would lose her job.

Louise was drawn to the religion of the Seventh Day Adventists, perhaps because their dietary regulations were in keeping with her own. They prohibited eating rabbit and pork as well as anything that didn't have a split hoof or chew a cud. Louise took the children to the prayer meetings. Malcolm especially enjoyed getting food to eat, although he and his siblings found it bland. At the time, Malcolm thought they were some of the nicest white people that he had met.

The welfare agents continued to harass Louise. They were incredulous when she refused free meat because it was pork. Her explanation that she was a Seventh Day Adventist meant nothing. Finally, the pain of losing her husband, being cheated by the insurance company, the grinding poverty and inability to keep a job because of her race and connection to Earl, and a sad ending to a new romance, pushed Louise over the edge. The state soon placed her in a mental institution in Kalamazoo, Michigan, and the children were assigned different homes.

RIGHT: Cross-burning was one method used by the Ku Klux Klan to terrorize black people.

LEFT AND BELOW LEFT: The old myth goes that lynching was used to discourage the rape of white women. In fact, it was used to discourage black people from succeeding in businesses and rebelling against white racists. In the 1920s and 1930s, the National Association for the Advancement of Colored People (NAACP) organized protests and memorials pressuring the U.S. president and vice president, as well as other legislators, for anti-lynching bills.

Malcolm lived in a series of foster homes. First he lived with a black family, the Gohannas, whom he really liked. However, after placing a tack on a teacher's seat at school, he was sent to a reform school in Mason, Michigan.

Malcolm was sent to live with the Swerlins, who ran the reform school. Malcolm was one of only two blacks in the home. While the Swerlins treated him nicely, they often spoke negatively about black people in his presence. This shocked and humiliated Malcolm.

Nevertheless, Malcolm achieved very good grades in Mason Junior High School. He enjoyed it tremendously, and was so popular that the students elected him class president.

Malcolm felt proud of his accomplishments. He saw little difference between himself as the lone black child and all the other children. An incident at school, however, would deeply disturb him. One day, after returning from a visit to see his half-sister Ella, who lived in the Roxbury section of Boston, his English teacher, a Mr. Ostrowski, took him aside and smilingly asked Malcolm if he had considered his future. Malcolm replied that he was considering becoming a lawyer. There was a long pause. Mr. Ostrowski leaned back and replied, "Malcolm, one of life's first needs is for us to be realistic . . . you've got to be realistic about being a nigger. A lawyer – that's no realistic goal for a nigger. You need to think about something you can be. You're good with your hands – making things . . . Why don't you plan on carpentry?"

Malcolm knew that students who received poorer grades than he, and who had much less ambition, were encouraged by the same teacher to be doctors or lawyers, teachers or nurses. Yet Mr. Ostrowski advised him to be a carpenter – because of his race.

LEFT: Jefferson School, later Mason High School, the school that Malcolm attended while living in Mason, Michigan.

LEFT: Ella Collins, Malcolm's half sister, as she appeared in 1965. Malcolm and Ella maintained a life-long connection. She arranged his move to Roxbury, Massachusetts, from Michigan, sent him money when he was imprisoned, and loaned him money for his trip to Mecca.

RIGHT: The "American Negro Exposition" opens in Chicago, 1940, and showcases black people's contributions to the U.S. in science, industry and the arts.

After that Malcolm withdrew inside himself. He glared whenever he heard a person say "nigger." He thought often about his recent visit to Roxbury. While there, Ella had introduced him to many black people who were widely travelled and well-versed in the ways of the world. He had listened to the music of Erskine Hawkins, Duke Ellington, Cootie Williams and many other black musicians, and felt at one with all the black people around him. For the first time in his life, Malcolm felt that he belonged somewhere.

Upon returning to Mason, Malcolm felt empty and alienated. The incident with Ostrowski made clear to him that Mason had nothing to offer him. His misery soon became apparent to all around him. The Swerlins were surprised by his change in attitude, and soon decided that they didn't want him to stay with them any longer. After a couple of transfers to other detention homes, Ella arranged for custody of Malcolm to be turned over to her.

Malcolm arrived in Roxbury to live with Ella in 1941.

Earl's daughter by his first marriage, Ella was a powerful woman, large and jet black. Malcolm recalled in his autobiography, "The way she sat, moved, talked, did everything, bespoke somebody who did and got exactly what she wanted." Malcolm remembered his father boasting that Ella had gone to Boston and made good. She had gone north with nothing, worked and saved and invested in property, then sent money south so her family could also travel north.

Malcolm arrived in Boston looking like a country boy. His kinky reddish hair was unfashionably close-cropped and ungreased. The coatsleeves of his green suit exposed his bony wrists, and his pants legs floated above his ankles. Even Ella shuddered at the sight of him.

Ella encouraged him to explore Boston before looking for work. He went all around the city, from the wealthy black section of Roxbury where Ella lived, to Cambridge, to the ghetto section of Roxbury where the poor black people lived. Malcolm disdained the wealthy black Rox-

bury residents because many of them put on airs. He despised the talk, "such and such is in banking," to describe someone who worked as a janitor in a bank. He preferred the poorer blacks living in the ghetto, who didn't pretend they were better than anybody else.

At a poolroom, Malcolm met "Shorty" Jarvis, who racked up balls for the pool players. As it turned out, Shorty was also from Lansing, and the two became friends. Shorty found Malcolm a job shining shoes at the Roseland State Ballroom on Massachusetts Avenue. The previous shoeshine, referred to in Malcolm's autobiography only as "Freddie," "schooled" him to everything he needed to know. He taught him to shine shoes, making the rag snap like a firecracker, explaining that the more of a show you put on for the white people, the more money you made. Malcolm quickly learned all the services that he could supply to the men in the Roseland washroom – liquor, "reefers" (marijuana cigarettes), white women for black men, black women for white men, condoms, and more. He didn't last long at the job, but he learned for the first time that, as Freddie had told him, "everything in the world is a hustle."

Hanging out with Shorty, Malcolm had his first taste of liquor, cigarettes, reefers, crap shooting, card playing, and daily betting on the numbers. Malcolm felt accepted and cared for by Shorty and his friends. It was Shorty who took Malcolm to buy his first "zoot suit," and who first "conked" or straightened his hair. Malcolm later recalled how pleased he was with his thick smooth sheen of shining red hair, "as straight as any white man's."

The Roseland was a dazzling ballroom, with wax floors and soft rose-colored lights that shone on the bandstand.

One night the dances were for whites, and another night for blacks. Malcolm learned to dance at the Roseland, and enthusiastically took to lindy-hopping, one of the favorite dances of the day. One of his favorite partners was a girl named Laura, whom he had met while working at a soda fountain in Sugar Hill, the wealthy black section of Roxbury. She lived with her strict grandmother, who didn't allow her to date, but the pair found ways to get together. Then one night at the Roseland, after dancing together in a

ABOVE AND LEFT: Duke Ellington and his band (ABOVE), Jimmie Lunceford and Chick Webb were some of the great black swing orchestras that played in Harlem's famous Savoy Ballroom (LEFT). The Savoy was also the site where popular dances such as the Susie Q, the Shag and the Lindy Hop got their start.

particularly energetic set, Malcolm felt the gaze of another woman – a white woman.

He turned to see Sophia, a striking woman whose desire shone plain in her eyes. Stricken, Malcolm took Laura home, then rushed back to the Ballroom to be with Sophia. Laura and Malcolm never dated again.

After leaving his job at the soda fountain, Malcolm began working on the Pullman train cars, loading supplies and selling sandwiches. His first job on the trains was on

the *Yankee Clipper*, which travelled from Boston to New York. Malcolm had heard about New York, and especially Harlem, but had never been there. He recalled his father's stories of Marcus Garvey's big parades trumpeting the uplift of the black race. Musicians at the Roseland had described Broadway's bright lights, the Savoy Ballroom, and the Apollo Theater in Harlem where the great bands played and the famous songs and dance steps and black stars originated. But none of these exciting descriptions

had prepared him for the glamorous reality.

As soon as he arrived in Harlem, Malcolm went to Small's Paradise, a black-owned club. He was stunned by the smoothness of the place, with its big, luxurious-looking circular bar. He stood awestruck by the quiet conservatism and finesse of the black men sitting at the bar. On that first trip, he also visited the Hotel Theresa, the finest hotel where black people could stay in the 1940s. Most of the fancy, downtown hotels refused accommodations to black people. Almost 20 years later, Malcolm was to meet with Fidel Castro at that very hotel.

By this time, Malcolm was running wild and staying high. He often went to work high on reefers. He detested many of the wealthy white customers on the train, and the white servicemen especially annoyed him. But already, Malcolm was honing his skills to outwit an opponent. He recalled an incident with a white serviceman who was very drunk, who stood in the middle of the aisle trying to start a fight with him. Laughing, Malcolm told the serviceman that he'd fight, but first he had to remove some of those clothes. The serviceman removed his overcoat. Malcolm said he still had on too many clothes. Soon the whole car was laughing, as the serviceman stood limply in the aisle, wearing nothing but his pants and shoes. His buddies led the drunk man away. Malcolm realized "that I couldn't have whipped that white man as badly with a club as I had with my mind."

After getting into spat after spat, Malcolm left the railroads for good. He soon found work as a waiter in Small's Paradise. Eager to make himself indispensable, he quickly ingratiated himself with the cooks and the customers. He also learned about Harlem and the hustling scene there. Some of the ablest of New York's black hustlers took a liking to Malcolm and knowing that he was new in town, began to "straighten Red out." But Small's wasn't only for hustlers. For the nightlife crowd, Small's was one of Harlem's two or three most genteel nightspots. New York City police frequently recommended Small's to white people

who were looking for a "safe" place to party in Harlem.

Nicknamed Detroit Red, Malcolm was learning all kinds of hustles. He stole fine suits with the Forty Thieves Gang, distributed bootleg whisky, bet on the numbers, and steered wealthy white men to prostitutes who would satisfy their every desire. He gradually adopted the hustlers' number one rule for survival – "you never trusted anyone outside of your own close-mouthed circle," and those you selected with care.

He even had a war resistance hustle. Like many black men in 1944, he saw no reason to fight for Uncle Sam, when Uncle Sam saw no reason to protect his life in the United States. So at the Army induction center he feigned craziness, looking under the draft official's desks, peering into corners, behaving as if someone was after him. Then he leaned over close to the psychiatrist and whispered that he couldn't wait until he got his gun, because he was going to be sure to kill some Southern "crackers." He didn't hear from the Army again for years.

Steering white men to prostitutes opened Malcolm's

LEFT AND BELOW LEFT: Small's Paradise was one of three night clubs for which Harlem was famous in the 1920s – the other two were Connie's Inn and the Cotton Club. While in Harlem, Malcolm became a waiter at Small's.

RIGHT: The Hotel Theresa, on 125th Street and Seventh Avenue in Harlem. In 1965, when Fidel Castro went to New York, he stayed at the Hotel Theresa, and met Malcolm X there.

BELOW: Black soldiers set sail for Liberia during World War II. Segregation within the army and discrimination at home made many blacks resent being sent to fight for the United States. Malcolm was just one of many men who came up with schemes to avoid being drafted.

eyes to the hypocrisy of white society. White men of all ages and classes sought favors from black prostitutes. He recalled in his autobiography: "Harlem was their sin-den, their fleshpot. They stole off among taboo black people, they took off whatever antiseptic, important, dignified masks they wore in their white world. These were men who could afford to spend large amounts of money for two, three, or four hours indulging their strange appetites."

Malcolm continued to date Sophia. From time to time she visited him in Harlem. Her beauty and whiteness impressed a lot of Malcolm's black buddies. When Sophia married a well-to-do Boston white man, she insisted that her relationship with Malcolm would go on just as before. One of Malcolm's friends, Sammy, had warned Malcolm that this might happen. Sammy explained that white women often married white men for money and security, while maintaining an affair with a black man out of pleasure and desire.

Malcolm bet so heavily on the numbers that he started placing bets with "West Indian Archie," who only

handled very large amounts of money. West Indian Archie had a photographic memory. Able to file all the numbers in his head, he never wrote down a number, even in combination plays. The only time he wrote down the numbers was for the banker when he turned in his money. This ensured that police couldn't catch West Indian Archie with any betting slips.

Men such as Archie made Malcolm acutely aware that the racist system wasted the potential of so many black people. "All of us – who might have probed space, or cured cancer, or built industries – were instead, black victims of the white man's American social system."

Drugs weakened his immune system. Smoking opium, and reefers almost by the ounce, he had colds constantly. He stayed so high, he lived in a dream world. Malcolm also sold reefers, and had an elaborate system set up whereby he could lose the evidence if he sensed that a policeman was following him. Living on the edge between awareness and oblivion, he tried to keep his wits about him.

Then one day, West Indian Archie came banging on the door of Sammy's apartment, where Malcolm was staying. Pointing a 32-20 caliber gun at Malcolm, he angrily accused Malcolm of cheating him out of $300 and demanded the money back. Malcolm swore that he had claimed the number that he played. He couldn't do otherwise – to give back the money would jeopardize his reputation among other hustlers, and his reputation was all a hustler had.

Archie left Sammy's warning Malcolm that he wanted his money by noon the next day. That night Malcolm foolishly went to one of his hangouts and sat with his back to the door, high as a kite. Next thing he knew, Archie was

standing before him, a gun in his hand, cursing. The only thing that saved him was Archie's friends who, softly calling his name, led Archie away.

Malcolm left the bar shaken. He kept expecting Archie to come for him, once the noon deadline passed, but he didn't. He spent much of the next day high, wandering the streets in a daze. Suddenly he heard a car drive up alongside him. Startled, he turned, his gun ready to fire. It was his friend Shorty, from Boston. Hearing that Red was in trouble, he had driven all the way to New York to take him back to Boston.

Back in Boston, Malcolm started a robbery ring with Shorty, Sophia, and her sister. The two women scouted the wealthy neighborhoods, touring the homes with ladies of the house. From the information gathered, they drew maps detailing the location of the valuables. The men stole the goods – rare Asian carpets, diamond rings, gold watches – often completing the job in as little as ten minutes. Rudy, another friend, drove the getaway car.

They made a lot of money for a time, and lived very well. Drugs helped Malcolm avoid recognizing that he was "walking on his own coffin." He was smoking reefers and taking cocaine every day to transcend any worries or cares. However, Malcolm later realized that his drug addiction was making him careless. One day he approached Sophia and her sister at a bar when they were out with Sophia's husband. He called the girls "baby." The next day, the brother came to Malcolm's house, looking for him.

Soon after, Malcolm was caught with a stolen watch. He and Shorty were sentenced to eight to ten years in prison; Sophia and her sister, three years each. Malcolm

LEFT: The corner of Dudley and Warren streets, the center of the Roxbury section of Boston, circa 1935. Malcolm was arrested in Boston and imprisoned in 1946.

RIGHT: At the age of 20, Malcolm was sentenced to Charlestown (Massachusetts) State Prison to serve an eight to ten year sentence.

BELOW: While in prison, Malcolm was introduced to the teachings of the Honorable Elijah Muhammad by his brother Reginald. Shown here is his brother Wilfred, who also converted to the Nation of Islam.

noted that eight years was a longer sentence than usual, but that he and Shorty had been penalized for "corrupting" the two white women as well.

Malcolm was sent to Charlestown State Prison in Boston in January 1946. The dirty, cramped cells didn't have running water. Covered pails were the only toilets, and the stench of feces permeated the cellblock. While there, he first got high on nutmeg, obtained from kitchen-worker inmates in exchange for money or cigarettes. Stirred into a glass of water, a tiny matchbox full of nutmeg provided the buzz of three or four reefers. Then with money from Ella, he bought reefers, nembutal, or benzedrine from the guards. Belligerent behavior earned him many hours in solitary confinement. For hours he would pace, his vicious cursing against the Bible and God earning him the nickname "Satan."

After a while, he noticed Bimbi, one of the inmates. About the same height and complexion as Malcolm, he was the first man Malcolm had seen in a long time who commanded respect with words. When Bimbi talked about history, the inmates would gather around and listen, transfixed. Bimbi suggested to Malcolm that he should use the prison library and take some correspondence courses to improve his writing. Encouraged by his sister Hilda, Malcolm began a couple of correspondence courses in English. Slowly he remembered his childhood grammar lessons. After a year, recalling Bimbi's discussions of word derivations, he began to study Latin.

As Malcolm's mind opened to the world of books, back in Detroit his family also embraced change. His brother Philbert sent a letter saying he had discovered the "natural religion for the black man." He belonged now to the "Nation of Islam." Because Philbert was always joining something, Malcolm was not remotely interested in his newest endeavor. Soon after, Reginald wrote, instructing Malcolm not to eat any pork or smoke any cigarettes. He ended by saying, "I'll show you how to get out of prison." Although he didn't know what kind of scheme Reginald was planning, he desperately wanted to get out of jail. He gave up cigarettes and pork.

Unknowingly, Malcolm had taken his first steps toward Allah.

In 1948, he was transferred to Norfolk (Massachusetts) Prison Colony, a heaven in comparison to Charlestown. It had flushing toilets, and walls instead of bars. In addition, each inmate had his own room. Intellectual stimulation ran high; instructors for the educational rehabilitation programs came from Harvard, Boston University and other educational institutions in the area. And the library was outstanding. The inmates were allowed to walk among the rows of books, selecting the ones they wanted.

When Malcolm entered Norfolk, he still didn't understand the majority of words that he was reading. This frustrated him terribly. Realizing that the best thing he could do was to study the dictionary, he began to do just that. Not certain where to begin, he began at the beginning, painstakingly copying each word, and its definition. Then, aloud, he read back everything he had written. Page by page, he eventually copied the entire dictionary.

All this time, Malcolm was heeding Reginald, refraining from smoking and eating pork. When Reginald finally came to see him, Malcolm anxiously awaited the plan to get out of jail. Reginald talked about the family, Detroit and many other things. Finally, he came to the point. He told Malcolm that there was a God walking among mortals, and his name was Allah. This God had been sent in the form of a black man by the name of Elijah Muhammad. Reginald explained that God has 360 degrees of knowledge, while the devil has only 33 degrees – this is Masonry. And the devil uses this Masonry to rule other people. "The devil is also a man," Reginald added. He gestured toward the white inmates and their visitors. "The white man is the devil."

When Reginald left, Malcolm's mind turned over and over. He thought about all the white people he had known: the state welfare people, his father's murderers, the employers who dismissed his mother when they learned she was Earl Little's wife, his English teacher's cutting remarks that a nigger could only be a carpenter, Sophia's husband's friend, and her husband, and on and on. Finally, he had an explanation for the treatment of his people by whites. They were devils. When Reginald returned a few days later, he told him about the "brainwashed black man." Reginald explained that the black man had come from ancient and highly evolved civilizations. But the devil white man had obscured all of that knowledge, and taught the black people to hate themselves. Furthermore, he continued, "You have been a victim of the evil of the devil white man ever since he murdered and raped and stole you from your native land in the seeds of your forefathers. . . ."

Malcolm began to receive letters daily from his brothers and sisters in Detroit. All had converted to the Nation of Islam. In their letters they referred to the Honorable Elijah Muhammad, the Divine Messenger of Allah, and urged Malcolm to accept his teachings.

Elijah Muhammad was born Elijah Poole in Sandersville, Georgia. One of thirteen children, Elijah was always

very small. As a young man, he spent hours poring over the Bible, so frustrated that he could not unlock its secret that tears shone in his eyes. He always had a strong sense of pride in being black, and could not stand how the Sandersville farmers would habitually and cruelly curse black workers.

He moved to Detroit with his new wife Clara, and it was there in 1931 that he met W.D. Fard, who was to become his spiritual leader. A light-skinned brown man with straight black hair, Fard sold silks and other beautiful fabrics door to door to black people in Detroit. He explained that he was born in the Koreish tribe of Muhammad ibn Abdullah, the Arabian prophet Himself. An expert on the Bible, he used the sale of his silks to get into black people's homes and tell them about their greatness. He revealed that blacks in America were directly descended from Muslims, and that they had been lost for 400 years from the Nation of Islam. He said he had been sent to awaken them to their true religion. Elijah was deeply affected by Fard's words, and became one of his first converts, and later, one of Fard's chosen. When Elijah asked Fard what his true identity was, Fard said he was the Messiah. Elijah became his supreme minister, and for three and a half years, until Fard disappeared, he received private teachings. Renamed Elijah Muhammad, he went on to create the Lost Found Nation, or the Nation of Islam.

Much of the power of the Nation of Islam's doctrine is that it holds the black man as central. As Malcolm thought over the teachings of Elijah Muhammad, he realized that there was a black man, a divine man, who understood the

meaning of his life, the meaning of all black people's lives; and that if he renounced the evil of his past, he too would know that meaning, and live a life rich with purpose, and justice. Deeply troubled by these thoughts, he could barely eat. At meal times, he just drank water. As he recalled in his autobiography, ''I was going through the hardest thing, also the greatest thing, for any human being to do; to accept that which is already within you, and around you.''

Starving for knowledge, Malcolm soaked up Elijah Muhammad's teachings, and ancient learning from the prison library. He read both Oriental and Occidental philosophers. He read Will Durant's *Story of Civilization*; H.G. Wells's *Outline of History*; W.E.B. DuBois's *Souls of Black Folk*, which talked of ancient African civilizations; Carter G. Woodson's *Negro History*, which described early African struggles for freedom; J.A. Rogers' *Sex and Race*, which outlined race mixing before the time of Christ. He went on to study genetics as described by Gregor Mendel. His eyes were opened to the horrors of slavery from reading books by Frederick Olmstead, Fannie Kimball, and Harriet Beecher Stowe. He studied Nat Turner's rebellion, and Herodotus, praised by Europeans as the "father of history." He learned how Europeans had plundered and ravished African nations for centuries. In these books, Malcolm found proof that "the collective white man had acted like a devil in virtually every contact that he had with the world's collective non-white man."

Malcolm also wrote daily to Elijah Muhammad, and Elijah answered his letters. Excited by his new awareness, Malcolm began trying to convert black inmates. Malcolm believed that the black inmate was among the ripest to accept the teachings of Elijah Muhammad and to accept that the white man is the devil, because he is caged behind bars, put there by the white man. "Usually the convict comes from among those bottom-of-pile Negroes, the Negroes who through their entire lives have been kicked about, treated like children – Negroes who never have met one white man who didn't either take something from them or do something to them. . . ." Malcolm believed that

when such a man is opened up to his potential, he would be a bitter man, but one who was ready for a change – ready to realize his power.

Malcolm signed up for the weekly debates in the Norfolk Prison Colony. He found debating exhilarating. Standing in front of the crowds, wracking his brain for facts to uphold his point and outwit his opponent, was a thrill. "I'd put myself in my opponent's place and decide how I'd try to win if I had the other side; and then I'd figure out a way to knock down those points." Whenever he could, he would work into those speeches the devilishness of the white man. "It was right there in prison that I made up my mind to devote the rest of my life to telling the white man about himself – or die."

Malcolm was transferred back to Charlestown, ostensibly for refusing to accept an inoculation. But it was becoming known that he was teaching about the Nation of Islam. He spent his last year in prison in Charlestown. Although supervision was stricter there, he still managed to spread the word of the teachings of Elijah Muhammad.

ABOVE LEFT: While in prison, Malcolm's mind was opened to the writings of many great thinkers. One of them was W.E.B. DuBois (center), shown here with Mary McLeod Bethune, founder of Bethune-Cookman College (Florida), and Horace Mann Bond, president of Lincoln University (Pennsylvania).

LEFT: W. E. B. Dubois, educator, scholar, writer and co founder of the NAACP, shown here at the offices of CRISIS, the magazine of the NAACP, which he edited from 1910 to 1934.

RIGHT: Malcolm was released from prison in 1952. Now a member of the Nation of Islam, he went on to spread the Nation's message that in America, no black person is free until he or she conquers the "habits and the vices, and the evils that hold them in the clutches of this white man's society."

In early September 1952, Malcolm joined a caravan of Muslims travelling to Chicago's Temple Number Two to hear the Messenger himself, Elijah Muhammad, speak. Malcolm was enchanted by his first glimpse of the Messenger, a delicately built man: "his sensitive, gentle, brown face . . . was fixed straight ahead as [he] strode, encircled by the marching, strapping Fruit of Islam guards." Muhammad electrified Malcolm with his words. To his surprise, Muhammad called his name, and right there before hundreds of people, he said that he believed in Malcolm, believed that the faith that he had adopted while in prison would remain with him, and that he would not return to his old ways of wasting away his life.

Inspired by the power of the Lost-Found Nation, Malcolm wanted to share it with other black people. He wanted to rescue them from their blind adoration of and dependence on the white man. Impatient with methods used by the Nation to gather converts, he began a recruitment campaign with Elijah Muhammad's blessings.

This came to be known as "fishing." Young Muslims went to Detroit ghetto bars, poolrooms, and street corners to find potential new converts. Most refused to heed their message, but the Muslims would find a few who would listen, and would beg them to come to Temple Number One for the next meeting. Many that promised didn't come. Out of the few that did, and that accompanied the

caravan to Chicago, few applied for membership. Even still, within a few months membership had tripled.

Eventually, Malcolm was encouraged by Lemuel Hassan, the minister of Temple Number Two, to address a couple of meetings of the congregation. Malcolm gave rousing speeches, and once again he realized how exciting speaking before a crowd was for him. In the summer of 1953, he was named Detroit Temple Number One's Assistant Minister.

At the Temple, Malcolm often addressed the place of

LEFT: Elijah Muhammad addresses followers on Savior's Day. To his right stands Sister Clara Muhammad, his wife.

BELOW LEFT: Elijah Muhammad wanted the Muslims of the Nation to realize their links with the "725 million brothers and sisters in the World of Islam." Shown here are members of the Federation of Islamic Associations.

RIGHT: Elijah Muhammad taught his followers to take pride in themselves, and made them aware that as black people they had a history that was ancient and honorable.

BELOW RIGHT: Black soldiers dine in a mess hall. The second time that Malcolm was approached by the Army, he applied for conscientious objector status.

the black man in American society. "We didn't land on Plymouth Rock, my brothers and sisters – Plymouth Rock landed on us!" He challenged black people's exaltation of their light skin, explaining the nature of slavery, and that the rape of black women by white slavemasters was a chief cause of the many different shades of skin. "Turn around and look at each other, brothers and sisters, and think of this! You and me, polluted with all these colors – and this devil has the arrogance and the gall to think we, his victims, should love him!"

While Malcolm was working for the Gar Wood auto factory, FBI agents visited the factory to find out why he hadn't registered for the draft. Malcolm pretended that he thought the government didn't accept ex-convicts. Then he went to the draft board, and filed for conscientious objector status.

As a rule, members of the Nation refused to fight for the United States, because their only allegiance was to the righteous wars declared by Allah. But Malcolm added a twist of his own to conscientious objector status. He told the reviewing officers that "when the white man asked me to go off somewhere and fight, and maybe die to preserve the way the white man treated the black man in America, then my conscience made me object." He soon received his deferred status.

A tremendous part of the belief of the Nation of Islam was pride, and Malcolm addressed that all the time. Time after time, the Nation transformed the poor and downtrodden black person, even the drug-addicted, into a powerful force, of use to himself, his family and his black nation. Self-determination was another important tenet of the Nation. Members were supported and encouraged to establish stores and other businesses. The Nation's modern bakery produced three types of bread, cakes, cookies and pies, and employed people as bakers, salesmen, and drivers. The grocery store was immaculate, and fully stocked with brand name foodstuffs.

The Nation also had an independent school system. The curriculum, from kindergarten to university, was geared to "free the so-called Negro from the teachings of his slavemasters." The curriculum focused on all issues relating to being black in America, as well as on traditional studies such as chemistry, physics, higher math, French, Spanish and Arabic. There was virtually no juvenile delinquency, thanks to the strict decorum maintained by parents, which provided a spotless model for living for their children.

Eventually, Malcolm left his job cleaning up after welders at the Gar Wood auto factory and went to work for the Ford Motor Company on the assembly line. By now, he was travelling to Chicago as often as he could to be with Elijah Muhammad. Mr. Muhammad treated him as if he were his son. He loved spending time with Elijah's wife, Clara, and Elijah's mother, whom he called Mother Marie.

In late 1953, Malcolm quit his job at the Ford Motor Company in order to devote himself full-time to "fishing" for souls and to establish more temples. For months, Elijah Muhammad personally groomed Malcolm for this task: "I was immersed in the worship rituals; in what he taught us were the true natures of men and women; the organizational and administrative procedures; the real meanings, and the interrelated meanings, and uses of the Bible and the Qur'an." Malcolm regarded Elijah with awe and adoration. Elijah was the first man that Malcolm ever feared, "the fear such as one has of the power of the sun."

Early in 1954, Malcolm was sent to Boston to start a Temple. Beginning in Brother Lloyd X's living room, Malcolm's fiery and inspiring teachings soon attracted enough new followers to open a little temple. While in Boston, Malcolm was reunited with his old friend Shorty. While in prison, Shorty had studied music and composition, and had started a small band. But he was not interested in Islam.

However, Malcolm's sister Ella started coming to hear Malcolm preach in Boston's new Temple Number Eleven. She eventually adopted the Nation of Islam. Malcolm only

LEFT: Elijah Muhammad also taught that black people should not fear whites. "I say to you that your fear of the white man is the Great Evil. Fear is of such a nature that it will make you deprive yourself of your own nature . . . . Fear is the real enemy . . . ." He also taught that white people would be destroyed because of their evil deeds, and that by choosing Islam, black people would be saved.

ABOVE RIGHT: The Nation of Islam set up schools (called "universities") for their children, where they learned African history and Arabic as well as traditional studies of math, science, and English. Photo shows police guarding Muhammad's Temple Number Two and the University of Islam in Chicago, Illinois, after Malcolm X's assassination in 1965.

RIGHT: A foundry worker at Ford Motor Company in Detroit, Michigan. Malcolm worked for Ford on their assembly line, but soon quit so as to devote himself full-time to spreading the teachings of Elijah Muhammad as the solution for the black man.

served a short time there. In March 1954, he left it under the charge of Minister Ulysses X, and moved to Philadelphia to spread the word.

Ripe for the message, Philadelphia had Temple Number Twelve by the end of May 1954. Extremely pleased with Malcolm's work, Elijah Muhammad assigned Malcolm to be minister of Temple Number Seven, in Harlem. Malcolm was overjoyed. He saw the enormous potential of New York, whose five boroughs contained over a million black people. At that time, Temple Number Seven was little more than a storefront. Few in Harlem knew what a Muslim was. Malcolm would change that.

Malcolm didn't have much success at first in getting people to join. He knew he had to get out in the streets that he remembered so well. At the time, the Nation of Islam was only one of numerous black nationalist groups seeking followers.

The Muslim brothers printed leaflets and passed them out on street corners. They ''fished'' on the edges of other nationalists' crowds. ''Come to hear us, too, brother. The Honorable Elijah Muhammad teaches us how to cure the black man's spiritual, mental, moral, economic, and political sicknesses. . . .''

They went to the Christian storefront evangelical churches. Malcolm was expert at tailoring his sermons for the audience. For the Christians, he explained how Christianity had brainwashed the black people. "Brothers and sisters, the white man has brainwashed us black people to fasten our gaze upon a blond-haired, blue-eyed Jesus! We're worshipping a Jesus that doesn't even look like us! . . . The white man has taught us to shout and sing and pray until we die, to wait until death, for some dreamy heaven-in-the-hereafter, when we're dead, while this white man has his milk and honey in the streets paved with golden dollars right here on this earth!" During the speeches, Malcolm would tell the people not just to believe what he was saying. He urged them to go look at where the white people lived, and to compare the conditions of their lives to the black people's lives. Then he would proclaim that Islam was a religion specifically for the black man.

While the nationalists tended to be men, the churchgoers were women. And Malcolm had something to say to them too. "Beautiful black women! The Honorable Elijah Muhammad teaches us that the black man is going around saying he wants respect; well, the black man never will get anybody's respect until he first learns to respect his own women!"

Even though they talked to a lot of people, and the people were interested, the strict moral code of the Lost-Found Nation repelled a lot of people. No drinking, no smoking, no drugs, no fornicating, only one meal a day, no pork. No dancing, no gambling, no dating, no attending movies or sporting events, no taking long vacations from work. No domestic quarrelling, no discourtesy, especially to women. No lying or stealing, no insubordination to civil authority, except on the grounds of moral obligation. And the militarily-trained Fruit of Islam enforced these codes. Infractions resulted in suspension by Mr. Muhammad, isolation, or even expulsion. Malcolm's brother Reginald was suspended for having an affair with the secretary of the New York Temple.

Despite setbacks, Temple Number Seven grew quickly. In addition to preaching six or seven nights a week at temple meetings and on Harlem street corners, Malcolm organized a nightly adult education course

BELOW LEFT: In February 1960, black students from North Carolina Agricultural and Technical State College protesting segregation staged a sit-in at the F.W. Woolworth lunch counter in Greensboro, NC, setting off a series of sit-ins across the country. Woolworth began desegregating its counters in July.

RIGHT: These Muslim women await the start of a speaking engagement by Elijah Muhammad in Indianapolis. Thousands of people would gather from around the country to hear Elijah Muhammad, or his powerful spokesman, Malcolm X.

BELOW: A crowd waits outside the Chicago Coliseum to hear Elijah Muhammad speak.

where he led debates about current events and religious topics. He travelled regularly to Philadelphia, Springfield (Massachusetts), Hartford (Connecticut) and Atlanta to preach in new temples there. By 1956, new temples had sprung up in Atlanta, Philadelphia, and Boston, and temples in Detroit, Chicago, and New York had sizeably increased membership.

By 1957, Malcolm was travelling to the West Coast and starting temples in Los Angeles and other western cities. He ultimately helped to create more than two dozen new congregations throughout the country.

Elijah Muhammad preached that "To integrate with evil is to be destroyed with evil." The Nation strived to create a separate black nation in America. They declared that the United States was obligated to grant the black people two to four states to run independently. Ultimately, all economic ties with whites were to be severed, and personal ties were to be cut immediately. The Nation forbade interracial marriages and integration in any context. The businesses begun by the Muslims were to enable the

Nation to separate economically as well. Followers did not vote, because they refused to participate in the political process.

Betty Shabazz was one of the sisters teaching the adult-education classes that Malcolm had started in Harlem. A nurse, she taught hygiene and health. Malcolm often sat in her classroom, watching her teach. While he also observed the other teachers, he found himself especially interested in Betty. The two of them spent many hours talking, and he liked her intelligence and quiet clarity. After a lot of thought, he decided that it would be a beneficial move for the Nation of Islam if he were to marry a woman of Betty's character. Once Malcolm received Elijah's OK to marry Betty, he called her up and proposed to her on the phone. They were married on January 14, 1958.

Many people were shocked when Malcolm married Betty. Although many of the women in Temple Number Seven were charmed by Malcolm, others had complained about Malcolm's harsh view of women. He often preached that women had led men to ruin, claiming that women

BELOW: Formerly Betty Sanders and a nurse, Betty X wed Malcolm X on January 14, 1958. Betty recalled tenderly that Malcolm would often hide gifts for her while he was travelling, then call and tell her where to look.

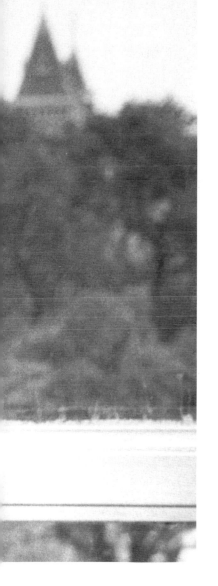

ABOVE: Malcolm X in Hartford, Connecticut. Malcolm constantly travelled around the country, setting up temples and teaching that the Nation of Islam was uniquely suited to meet the needs of the 22 million black people of America, and would enable them to achieve financial, physical and mental independence.

"were only tricky, deceitful, untrustworthy flesh." In an address at the Philadelphia Temple, Malcolm accused black women of being the greatest tool of the devil, saying that black men had gotten into such a terrible state because of "our women tricking him and tempting him, and the devil taught her how to do this."

Later in his life, Malcolm altered these views, no doubt because of his strengthening relationship with Betty. When he returned from Africa and the Middle East years later, he related that women played a key role in liberation struggles there, and that the progress of a nation cannot be separated from the progress of its women.

The FBI began investigating the Nation and even infiltrating it as early as 1953. Malcolm stated that no fewer than fifteen agents were regularly assigned to cover his New York Temple alone. It was later revealed that the FBI had kept extensive records on the Nation of Islam, and on Malcolm X, for years.

Until 1957, the Nation was not widely known about by white people. But an incident of police brutality that year changed that. It started with police beating a black suspect on a Harlem street corner. Hinton Johnson, a member of the Nation who was observing this, shouted out to the police, "You're not in Alabama – this is New York!" The police ordered him away. He refused, and they started clubbing him too, and then arrested him.

While this was not the first confrontation between black people and the police in Harlem, it was the first time that the Nation had gotten involved. One of the brothers reported to the Temple that Hinton was in the round-house. In less than half an hour, about 50 of Temple

Seven's Fruit of Islam were standing in ranks-formation outside the police precinct house. Other black people, curious, gathered behind them. James Hicks, editor of Harlem's weekly, the *Amsterdam News*, and mediator between the police and the Muslims, estimated that there were at least 2500 people gathered outside the police station. The police were flabbergasted, and afraid. Malcolm made clear that the people would not leave the station until Hinton Johnson was seen. The police gave in. Malcolm was shocked at the sight of the badly beaten

ABOVE LEFT: Malcolm and Betty at the hearing of 14 Muslims who were shot by police in LA in 1962.

LEFT: James Hicks (left), editor of the *Amsterdam News*, acted as mediator between Malcolm and the police after Hinton Johnson, a member of the Nation, was severely beaten by the police in 1957.

ABOVE: Mike Wallace (left) produced and narrated the 1959 television program "The Hate That Hate Produced."

RIGHT: Outspoken black reporter Louis Lomax (right) conducted interviews with Malcolm X and Elijah Muhammad for the program. Here he is shown interviewing Dr. Alberto Chassagne of Haiti in 1958.

Johnson, bathed in blood, his skull gaping open. After demanding that the police call for an ambulance, Malcolm walked outside and thanked the crowd for their support. Explaining that all that could be done had been, he waved them away. And the crowd dispersed. One of the police people was so amazed at the hold that Malcolm had over the crowd that he breathed, "This is too much power for one man to have." Hicks thought to himself, "He means one black man."

In 1959 Louis Lomax, the first black man to appear on

TV as a reporter, was assigned by Mike Wallace to investigate Harlem's black nationalists. In the course of his research, he was advised to look into the Nation of Islam, whose leading spokesman was Malcolm X. That led to many conversations with Malcolm X, then conversations with Elijah Muhammad and numerous meetings at the Temple. The resulting story, produced and narrated by Mike Wallace, was called "The Hate That Hate Produced." The airing of the show in late 1959 provided the Nation of Islam with national coverage. For the first time,

RIGHT: On August 28, 1963, 250,000 people led by Dr. Martin Luther King marched from the Washington Monument to the Lincoln Memorial. Malcolm vehemently opposed the march. He viewed it as a farce because originally, thousands of poor black people had intended to march on Washington demanding jobs and economic opportunity. He believed that civil rights leaders had allowed the march to be diluted when they changed the direction to marching for freedom and integration.

whites in the United States had an inside view of the Nation of Islam, and heard for themselves that the Nation viewed them as a race of white devils whose nature is evil, and that the black man is by nature divine. Mike Wallace was clearly upset by what he interpreted as black people returning white people's hatred and violence with hatred and violence. In his closing statements, he pressed black and white audiences to support the nonviolent movement to racially integrate the United States.

The program was especially shocking in the context of the burgeoning civil rights movement. In 1954, the Supreme Court had decreed that "separate but equal" is inherently unequal. In 1955, Rosa Parks refused to surrender her seat to a white passenger on a Montgomery, Alabama, bus, thereby igniting the Montgomery Bus Boycott. The boycott catapulted Martin Luther King, Jr. into public view. Many people were turning to King, inspired by his message of nonviolence. King took the moral high ground, appealing to the best in humanity.

Malcolm offered no such hope. As the spokesman for

the Nation of Islam, he espoused separation from white people – not integration. When asked if he was preaching hate, he replied, "How can anybody ask us do we hate the white man who kidnapped us 400 years ago, brought us here and stripped us of our history, stripped us of our culture, stripped us of our language, stripped us of everything you could have used today to prove you're a part of the human family, bring you down to the level of an animal, sell you from plantation to plantation like a sack of wheat, sell you like a sack of potatoes, sell you like a horse and a

plow, and then hung you up from one end of the country to the other, and then you ask me do I hate him? . . . Why, your question is worthless."

Malcolm drew on his own life experiences to condemn the concept of integration. As far as he was concerned, integration was a farce. In one of his speeches, he laughingly said he loved to talk about white people like dogs, and they should be able to take it. "Why, when I was a little boy, they called me nigger so much, I thought that was my name." Malcolm saw it as only fair that whites should

father. Betty Shabazz later said that Malcolm had not really known his father, and the relationship that Malcolm had forged with Elijah was a very special one. But it did not last. Years before, Elijah had warned Malcolm that there were those who may become jealous. Malcolm ignored the warnings. He did not heed rumors that there were officials in the Nation who believed that he was getting too big for the Nation, that he thought he was more important than Elijah Muhammad, that Malcolm was plotting to take over the Nation.

The way in which Malcolm handled his financial affairs indicates that he had no such plans. When Elijah Muhammad advised him to accept as a gift the house he was living in, Malcolm refused. When Betty expressed concern that they did not have money put away, he told her not to worry, for the Nation would take care of her should anything happen to him.

Just as many members of the Nation were uneasy with Malcolm's growing popularity, he was becoming uncomfortable with the Nation's policy of political noninterven-

LEFT: A rally is held in New York in 1963 to protest the arrest of black Muslims for the sale of the newspaper *Muhammad Speaks* on 42nd Street.

BELOW: Malcolm with politicians Adam Clayton Powell (left) and Hulan Jack, the first black borough president in New York City, at a rally in Harlem in 1963.

ABOVE: Police look down from the top of a nearby building as Malcolm addresses a crowd in Harlem in June 1963.

RIGHT: The crowd listens as Malcolm speaks.

FAR RIGHT: Malcolm speaks at a Harlem rally on June 15, 1963, in support of integration efforts in Birmingham, Alabama. A. D. King, Martin Luther King's younger brother, also spoke that day, two days after his home had been bombed by racists in Birmingham, who were adamantly against integration.

Muhammad forbade Malcolm to organize any protests or calls for vengeance. He did not want the Nation of Islam held responsible for any riots or bloodshed that could be linked with the event. Malcolm desperately wanted to do something, so he went to LA and presided over the funeral. He took pictures of Stokes, blew them up to wall size and used them at rallies, pointing to the holes and grooves in Stokes's head to illustrate the police brutality. He also released these pictures to the *Amsterdam News* and a few other papers.

Malcolm was sharply criticized for a comment that he made out of anger soon after that. A charter jet crashed in France, carrying many members of the white cultural elite of Atlanta. Malcolm declared that it served them right: "I love to see bad things happen to them." He claimed Allah was punishing them for their sins.

Such comments were callous. But he was voicing the hatred that black people felt toward white people, hatred that had been nurtured and fed for hundreds of years. And Malcolm believed that not admitting that hatred, profess-

ing only love as Martin Luther King did, would not help the majority of black people to heal from the wrongs inflicted on them.

After the Stokes incident, a close friend of Malcolm's, Benjamin Karim, noted that Malcolm began to speak less for the Nation and more for himself.

Malcolm received a major shock when he learned that Elijah Muhammad had fathered children by at least six of his secretaries. Malcolm had heard whispers of this, but he ignored them. He did not want to believe that the man he

loved as a father and worshipped as a god was a hypocrite. But the time came when Malcolm could not hide from the truth any longer. He travelled to Arizona to ask the Divine Messenger about the rumors. Elijah said they were true, and explained to Malcolm that as one of prophets in the line of David he was doing what they had done, by committing adultery. It was all written; it was destiny.

Malcolm wanted to believe this at first, as he did not want to question the wisdom of the Divine Messenger. However, the more he thought about it, the more he

LEFT: The assassination of President John F. Kennedy on November 22, 1963, stunned the nation. Stores closed, and people, black and white, grieved. On December 1, 1963, Elijah Muhammad asked Malcolm to speak in his place, and Malcolm spoke on ''God's Judgement of White America.'' In the speech he said that ''the seeds that America had sown — in enslavement, in many things that followed since then — all these seeds were coming up today; it was harvest time.'' It was after this speech that he commented that John Kennedy's assassination was a case of ''chickens coming home to roost.''

RIGHT: Women waiting outside Parkland Hospital in Dallas weep upon learning of President Kennedy's death.

RIGHT: On May 16, 1963, Malcolm had criticized President Kennedy's and Attorney General Robert Kennedy's handling of the racial situation in Birmingham, Alabama. ''President Kennedy did not send troops to Alabama when dogs were biting black babies. He waited three weeks until the situation exploded. He then sent troops after the Negroes had demonstrated their ability to defend themselves.''

thought that in order to confront any other rumors, he should search for biblical evidence that the deeds of the man outweigh any personal failings. He shared his shock with his wife. He also shared it with some others in the Nation. This would prove to be a mistake, for some of them sent in reports to Chicago that Malcolm was spreading false rumors. The trap was set.

In 1963, John F. Kennedy was shot. All of the ministers of the Nation of Islam were ordered to refrain from discussing the assassination. On December 1, 1963, Elijah cancelled an engagement to speak at Manhattan Center, and asked Malcolm to go for him. During his speech, Malcolm did not comment on the assassination at all, but in the question and answer period he was asked what he thought about it. Malcolm, not one to say "no comment," replied that it was a case of "the chickens coming home to roost," "and being an old farm boy myself, chickens coming home to roost never did make me sad, they've always made me glad." From Malcolm's point of view, Kennedy's foreign and domestic policies had led to their natural outcome. And that's what he said.

Elijah Muhammad silenced Malcolm for 90 days as a result of that comment. However, even after 90 days, he did not lift the suspension. During his silence, Malcolm slowly realized Elijah Muhammad had been displeased with him for a while. Ensnared by his own words, Malcolm had hastened the Nation's plan to cut him loose.

ABOVE: Malcolm stressed that black people know that their history was rooted in the advanced ancient civilizations of Egypt, Mali, Ghana and Songhai, among others.

RIGHT: Malcolm with his third daughter, Ilyasah, named after Elijah Muhammad.

Nation, he was open to acknowledging whatever he saw, thirsty to receive new knowledge and enhanced understanding.

On April 13, 1964, Malcolm set out for Mecca. He was, however, not allowed to enter immediately. Officials questioned whether he was an authentic convert, since only true Muslims were allowed to enter Mecca. He had to wait to go before the Mahgama Sharia, the Muslim high court which examined all possible nonauthentic converts to the Islamic religion seeking to enter Mecca.

From the airport, he called a friend of a friend, Omar Azzam. Azzam rushed to the airport, and in a matter of minutes they were on the way to Azzam's home. Azzam, a tall, powerfully built young man, was a Swiss-trained engineer in charge of rebuilding all of the Arabian holy sites. He was also the brother-in-law of the ruler of Saudi Arabia, King Faisal. Azzam's father, Abd ir-Rahman Azzam, was an Egyptian-born Saudi citizen, an international statesman, and one of Prince Faisal's closest advisors.

Azzam's generosity moved Malcolm nearly to tears. Azzam, by all appearances a white man, insisted Malcolm stay in his luxurious hotel suite while he awaited permission to enter Mecca. Malcolm groped for an ulterior motive to explain Azzam's kindness, but he found none.

Slowly Malcolm began to suspect that "white" as he knew it within the United States was a state of mind, a set of attitudes. Not once during his lengthy conversations with Azzam did he feel that he was interacting with someone who considered himself a superior.

Finally allowed to enter Mecca, Malcolm went humbly. As is the custom, he doffed his worldly clothes, and entered Mecca wrapped in two white cloths. A pair of simple sandals covered his feet. So dressed, all men become equal – whether a king or a pauper, all appear the same before Allah.

Surrounded by 50,000 devotees of Allah, of all races, colors, and nationalities, men and women, Malcolm joyously made his way to the sacred Ka'aba. A huge black stone house in the middle of the Great Mosque, the Ka'aba is said to have fallen from the heavens. Malcolm circled the Ka'aba seven times, trying to get close enough to kiss the sacred stone. The crowds were overwhelming, so, raising his hand toward the stone, and filled with holy rapture, he called out "Takbir! Takbir!" (God is great!).

Deeply moved by his experience of Islam as a religion of true brotherhood, Malcolm could not keep it to himself.

been so touched by Ghanaian independence that they had come to support the government and its president, Kwame Nkrumah, with their many skills and talents. The Malcolm X Committee, formed of these expatriates, guided Malcolm through Ghana, organizing meetings and social events.

At one of the many speeches that Malcolm delivered in Ghana, a young man stood up and asked Malcolm why he called himself black, since he appeared more white than black. Malcolm laughed long and loud. Commending the young man for having the courage to ask what he was certain many had thought, he explained that whites in America had never tried to claim him. He explained that during the time of slavery, white slavemasters had raped and enslaved Africans with impunity and refused to claim the offspring. But the African women claimed their off-

He began to write letter after letter – to Betty, to Ella, to his followers at the Muslim Mosque, to the press. He described his experiences during the past 11 days in Mecca, eating from the same plate, drinking from the same glass, and sleeping on the same rug with fellow Muslims, whose hues ranged from the whitest white to the blackest black. ''We were truly all the same (brothers) – because their belief in one God had removed the 'white' from their minds, the 'white' from their behavior, and the 'white' from their attitude.''

Malcolm was now convinced that if Americans could accept the Oneness of God, then perhaps they too could truly accept the Oneness of Man, ''and cease to measure, and hinder, and harm others in terms of their 'differences' in color.'' The experience made Malcolm whole. ''In my 39 years on this earth, the Holy City of Mecca had been the first time I had ever stood before the Creator of All and felt like a complete human being.''

From Mecca, he flew to Beirut, Lebanon, then to Lagos, Nigeria. In Lagos, he appeared on radio and television, and spoke before hundreds of students. Young people of the Nigerian Muslim Students' Society made him an honorary member, and gave him the name ''Omowale,'' Yoruba for ''the son who has come home.''

From Lagos, he travelled to Accra, Ghana, where he stayed with African-American author Julian Mayfield. Ghana was host to many African-Americans who had

While in Africa, Malcolm met with Kwame Nkrumah (in suit), shown here with his Egyptian-born wife. Nkrumah was the first president of Independent Ghana. Malcolm spoke reverently of his time spent discussing Pan-Africanism and its applications to black Americans.

FAR LEFT AND LEFT: During the 90 days that Malcolm was silenced by the Nation, boxer Cassius Clay invited Malcolm and his family to Florida to provide spiritual guidance as he trained to fight Sonny Liston. Clay's sound defeat of Liston made him heavyweight champion of the world. The day after the victory, he announced that he was a member of the Nation of Islam, and was to be called Muhammad Ali.

RIGHT: In Tanganyika (now Tanzania) in October 1964, Malcolm met with Minister of State Abdul Rahman Babu, who later visited Malcolm in the United States.

BELOW: In Cairo, Egypt, Malcolm meets with Sheik Abdel Rahman Tag (right), future rector of Al Azhar, the only Muslim university in the world. Malcolm was anxious to make certain that his new Muslim Mosque would be considered orthodox.

spring. He observed that that legacy continued, as whites refused to claim their links with African-Americans.

While in Ghana, Malcolm sought support for his plan to bring the case of African-Americans before the United Nations. He met with Ghanaian Cabinet Ministers, the African and European Diplomatic Corps and Cuban and Chinese ambassadors. He also met with Dr. Kwame Nkrumah, which he described as his highest single honor.

When Malcolm returned from Africa, having taken the name El-Hajj Malik El Shabazz, the media was waiting for him, and so were his followers. Whites emphasized his increased tolerance for them. But many of his black followers, uncertain of his direction, felt betrayed.

Malcolm remained firm. He would no longer be placed in an ideological straitjacket. "I'm for truth, no matter who tells it. I'm for justice, no matter who it is for or against. I'm a human being first and foremost, and as such I'm for whoever and whatever benefits humanity as a whole."

He returned to the United States determined to take the case of blacks in America before the United Nations.

ABOVE AND LEFT: Upon his return from Africa and the Middle East, Malcolm founded the non-secular Organization of African-American Unity, inspired by Ghana's Organization of African Unity. The 17-point plan of the OAAU included creation of schools run by the Afro-American community, political clubs to sponsor independent candidates, and improved housing. Here he addresses an OAAU meeting.

John F. Kennedy had passed the Civil Rights Bill, but Malcolm found it woefully inadequate. Instead of pleading for civil rights, he wanted blacks in America to see the injustices committed against them as human rights violations. "Human rights! Respect as human beings. That's what America's black masses want. . . . They want not to be walled up in slums, in the ghettoes, like animals. They want to live in an open, free society where they can walk with their heads up, like men and women!"

On June 24, 1964, Malcolm announced the formation of the secular Organization of African American Unity (OAAU). Inspired by his encounters with members of the Pan-Africanist Organization of African Unity (OAU), the OAAU's 17-point program expressed a revolutionary self-defense and nation-building plan for blacks within the United States. The OAAU stated that, while blacks in America might remain physically in America, culturally and psychologically they needed to "return" to Africa, and to view themselves in solidarity with Africans.

Malcolm wanted blacks to realize that just because

they were the minority in America, they were not the minority in the world. In South, Central and North America alone, there were 80 million people of African descent. Furthermore, Africans looked sympathetically on the plight of African-Americans. He encouraged blacks in the United States to examine what was truly meant by a revolution, and to learn from Africa's successful independence movements.

Later that year, Malcolm made a third trip to Africa, during which he spent days meeting with African heads of state. While in Cairo, Egypt, he attended the African Sum-

ABOVE: Adam Clayton Powell (left) and Malcolm talk before the March 16, 1964 boycott of New York public schools. A total of 165,000 students stayed out of school protesting segregation in the schools.

RIGHT: Malcolm attends a session of the New York State Legislature in Albany on January 6, 1965.

OVERLEAF: On February 14, 1965, Malcolm's home was firebombed while he and his family slept. Here, he arrives at his home the following day.

mit Conference as a representative of OAAU. He appealed to delegates of the 34 African nations to bring the cause of black people of the U.S. to the U.N. He did not receive the explicit commitments that he needed, though, largely because of what he termed "dollarism." Many newly independent African nations were looking to the United States for financial aid and development assistance. They could not afford to speak out too harshly. But he did succeed in alerting Africans to the subhuman conditions in which many blacks in America were forced to live. Now U.S. ambassadors to Africa found themselves forced to explain why the violence and racism that Malcolm had so vividly described was allowed to endure.

Malcolm also conferred with senior officials of the Al Azhar Islamic Center. From them he received certification as an orthodox Sunni Muslim minister, and was able to link his Muslim Mosque, Inc. with the world's 750 million orthodox Muslims.

In a conversation with writer Maya Angelou, he equated the nature of racism to a mountain. When that mountain is cut from top to bottom, the many layers represent the layers of racism. To tear down that mountain, different people must work on different levels. New insights such as these made Malcolm more tolerant to the variety of perspectives of civil rights leaders, although he never supported non-violence. In his desire to join together all black groups that were fighting for justice for blacks in America, he publicly apologized to those civil rights leaders that he had insulted and asked that they forget everything uncomplimentary that he had said about them.

He also spoke out about political representation. He said that if black people decided to participate in the political system, and to vote, then they must hold politicians accountable. And if they voted for politicians who did not deliver, then the next time, instead of a ballot, they should cast a bullet. He warned that 1964 would be a bloody year, for young people did not want to hear about "turning the other cheek." They wanted to see a democracy that represented them – and if they didn't, they would resort to terrorist tactics, and be justified in doing so.

Meanwhile, Malcolm knew that his life was in danger. Unidentified black men trailed him constantly. At home, his phone rang often with threats against his life. At first Malcolm believed that the Nation of Islam was behind all of the threats on his life. However, on his return from Africa via Europe, France refused him entrance. Stunned, he realized that the forces conspiring against him were larger than the Nation – that, in fact, the Central Intelligence Agency (CIA) was probably involved.

Malcolm saw a violent death as inevitable. Although he was offered positions in Africa that would have ensured safety for himself and his family, he refused them. He believed that while such a move would solve his personal problems, it would do nothing for the millions of black people that he represented.

On the morning of February 14, 1965, four Molotov cocktails were hurled into Malcolm's home while he and his family slept. Left homeless, Betty and the four children stayed with friends, while Malcolm stayed in a hotel. On the morning of February 21, 1965, he was awakened by a phone call. A voice, belonging to a white man, said, "Wake up, brother."

Malcolm was due to speak at the Audubon Ballroom that day. Several weeks before, he had ordered that security checks of attendees be stopped, saying, "If I can't be safe among my own kind, where can I be?"

Friends who saw him at the Ballroom described him as restless and anxious. He even felt that he should forego speaking. After the half-hour introduction by Benjamin Karim, Malcolm stepped out to the podium. "As-Salaam-Alaikum," he said. The audience of 400 answered, "Wa-Alaikum-Salaam." Suddenly, an argument broke out. Malcolm called for calm. In that instant, three men stood up and opened fire on him. Doctors pronounced Malcolm dead upon arrival at the hospital.

The three men found guilty of his death – Talmadge Hayer, Norman 3X Butler, and Thomas 15X Johnson, all members of the Nation of Islam – were sentenced to life imprisonment. However, recent evidence shows that probably only one of the three, Hayer, actually shot Mal-

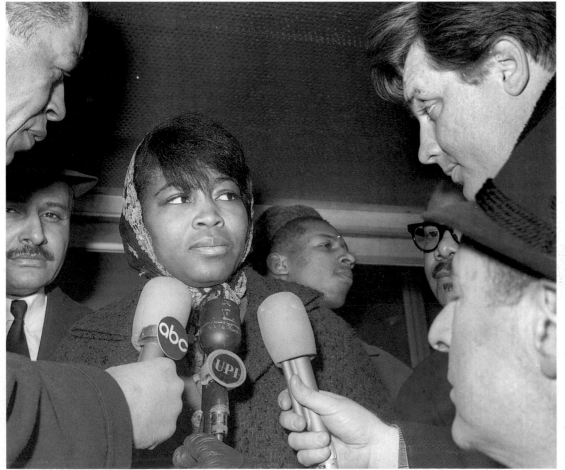

ABOVE: A marcher carries a sign saying, ''He didn't die in vain'' outside of the Unity Funeral Home, where Malcolm's body is on view. Malcolm was then dressed as an orthodox Sunni Muslim and taken to Faith Temple.

LEFT: Betty Shabazz with state legislator and lawyer Percy Sutton (left) answers questions from reporters.

ABOVE AND LEFT: Actor Ossie Davis delivers the eulogy for Malcolm at Faith Temple (ABOVE) while thousands gather outside to pay their last respects (LEFT).

colm. The other men involved have never been caught.

While brothers from the Nation of Islam may have pulled the trigger, what other forces were involved in hastening Malcolm's end? FBI memos boasting that FBI agents in Chicago had developed the murderous feud between Malcolm and Elijah Muhammad have recently been unearthed. Certainly the FBI had trailed and infiltrated the Nation and Islam for years. During the 1960s, one in five members of the Fruit of Islam may have been FBI agents or informers. And what of Malcolm's realization when he

was refused entry to France that something bigger than the Nation of Islam was involved? Only meticulous investigation will reveal the full truth.

On February 22, 1965, 20,000 people lined up around the block to say goodbye to the 39-year-old Malcolm, as he lay in the Unity Funeral Home in Harlem. Four days later, Sheik Ahmed Hassoun Jaaber removed Malcolm's Western clothes, and anointed and dressed the body as an Orthodox Sunni Muslim. He was buried in Ferncliff Cemetery in Westchester, NY, his body facing east.

Every Goodbye Ain't Gone

Malcolm is still with us. Even during the 1970s, when only black nationalists saw value in his words and young people wondered why they should study Malcolm "Ten," he was with us.

His newly found popularity is ironic. When he was killed, the mainstream media couldn't crow loudly enough. The *New York Times* blamed Malcolm for his own death, calling him a "twisted man, with a ruthless and fanatical belief in violence." *Time* magazine called him "an unashamed demagogue" whose "gospel was hatred" and who "in life and in death – was a disaster to the Civil

PAGE 74: Betty Shabazz with filmmaker Spike Lee (left) and Ossie Davis in 1992. Today Betty is the director of communications and public relations at Medgar Evers College in Brooklyn, New York.

PREVIOUS PAGE: Betty Shabazz after a 1966 service held in memory of Malcolm in Los Angeles.

LEFT: Denzel Washington as Malcolm X, in the critically acclaimed 1992 film *Malcolm X*, directed by Spike Lee.

BELOW: Angela Bassett portrayed Betty Shabazz in *Malcolm X* (1992).

RIGHT: Hairstyles are one symbol of renewed interest in Malcolm X. Here, Ralph Wilburn applies finishing touches to Christopher Shepherd's haircut.

Rights movement.'' Even the African-American media acidly remarked that he had reaped what he had sown, and that death was his just desserts.

Malcolm would not have been surprised at their words. ''They call it hate teaching, but I call it love teaching. 'Cause I wouldn't tell you if I didn't love you.''

Spike Lee's 1992 film *Malcolm X* has helped bring alive Malcolm's love teachings and to show him as a man, with frailties and strengths, a man who embraced sweeping changes, to arrive whole before his Creator.

As African-Americans reflect on the changes wrought by the civil rights movement, many question how much progress was really made. The defanging of civil rights legislation, the criminalization of black men and never-ending funds allocated to prisons instead of to education and health, leave a generation after the 1960s watching dreams crumble like dust. Malcolm's bitter disdain for legislative actions echo sharply.

But it is not enough to remember Malcolm's disdain. He also left a ringing call for truth. In his last year, he was shaping a new vision of what a grassroots movement must do to gain justice. A key aspect of that was the demand that blacks and whites face the truth of where the United States was heading. He warned that it would not be long before the violence that had been sown would lead to yet more violence, and this time, the bleeding would be reciprocal.

But he offered a solution: for whites to abide by their own laws, not to discriminate based on the color of a person's skin, and to commit wholeheartedly to a true democracy; and for blacks to demand that their rights be upheld, and that justice be for all. In this, Malcolm saw the key to America's survival.

Nearly 30 years later, Malcolm's words ring as loud and clear as ever. It is clear that America's survival is still in jeopardy.

LEFT: Many new books about Malcolm X have recently been published including his speeches as well as reassessments of his life and death. Here, Taka Haggins reads a Malcolm X biography at the Truth bookstore in Philadelphia.

Index

Bibliography

Malcolm X Speaks, Selected Speeches and Statements, edited with prefatory notes by George Breitman, Grove Press, NY © 1965.

Malcolm X: The Man and His Times, by John Henrik Clarke, © 1969 First Collier Books Edition, and reprinted © 1990 First World Africa Press, Inc.

Martin & Malcolm & America: A Dream or a Nightmare, by James H. Cone, Orbis Books, Maryknoll, NY, © 1991.

The Autobiography of Malcolm X: As told to Alex Haley, © 1964 by Alex Haley and Malcolm X, © 1965 by Alex Haley and Betty Shabazz, Ballantine Books, NY.

The Black Muslims in America, by C. Eric Lincoln, Beacon Press Books, © 1961.

To Kill a Black Man: The Shocking Parallel in the Lives of Malcolm X and Martin Luther King, Jr., by Louis E. Lomax, Holloway House Publishing, © 1968, 1987.

The Death and Life of Malcolm X, by Peter Goldman, Harper and Row, NY, © 1973, 1979.

Acknowledgements

Thank you to Bryn Clark, my husband, who talked and debated with me for hours as I learned about Malcolm's life, and who read the manuscript as it developed. Thank you to Michael Simmons and Zoharrah Simmons who shared their personal histories as civil rights workers, and people who experienced Malcolm during that time. And thank you to Aishah Simmons and Midori Lockett who read the manuscript and shared what it unearthed for them. And a special thank you to all my wonderful friends who challenge me to live up to my full potential. Thanks also to those who were involved with the preparation of this book: Sara Dunphy, the picture editor; Jean Martin, the editor; Alan Gooch of Design 23, the designer; Nicki Giles for production; and Elizabeth A. McCarthy, the indexer.

Picture Credits